T0160920

NIGHTBOAT BOOKS, NEW YORK

JEN BERVIN

SILK POEMS

© 2017 JEN BERVIN

ALL RIGHTS RESERVED

PRINTED IN THE UNITED STATES

ISBN 978-1-937658-72-4

DESIGN BY QUEMADURA

TEXT SET IN INTERSTATE AND MRS. EAVES

COVER AND INTERIOR ART BY JEN BERVIN

CATALOGING-IN-PUBLICATION DATA IS AVAILABLE

FROM THE LIBRARY OF CONGRESS

DISTRIBUTED BY UNIVERSITY PRESS OF NEW ENGLAND

ONE COURT STREET

LEBANON, NH 03766

WWW.UPNE.COM

NIGHTBOAT BOOKS

NEW YORK

WWW.NIGHTBOAT.ORG

"The wiggle of a worm as important as the assassination of a president."

AGNES MARTIN

It is said that silk filature began in China under a mulberry tree in a teacup resting lightly in the slender hand of the empress Hsi-ling shi. A brin unfurls from the frisson tangle. She reaches in, begins to reel filament from the soft envelope of the cocoon. That is how people like to tell it.

You know the Nigerian proverb—until the lions have their own historians, history will always be told by the hunters.

If you don't know it
why not

S

O
P
K
L
I
S
M
E

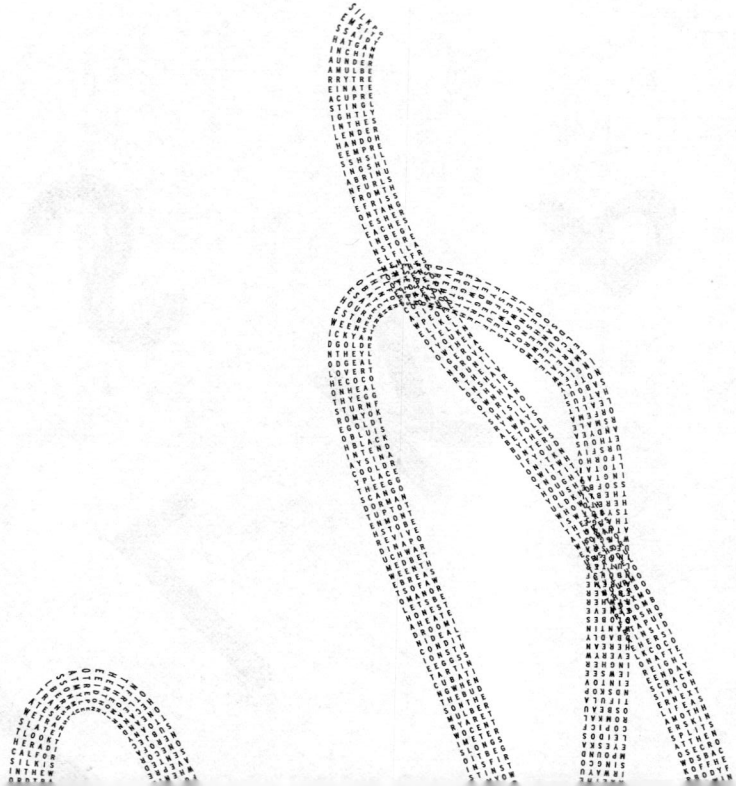

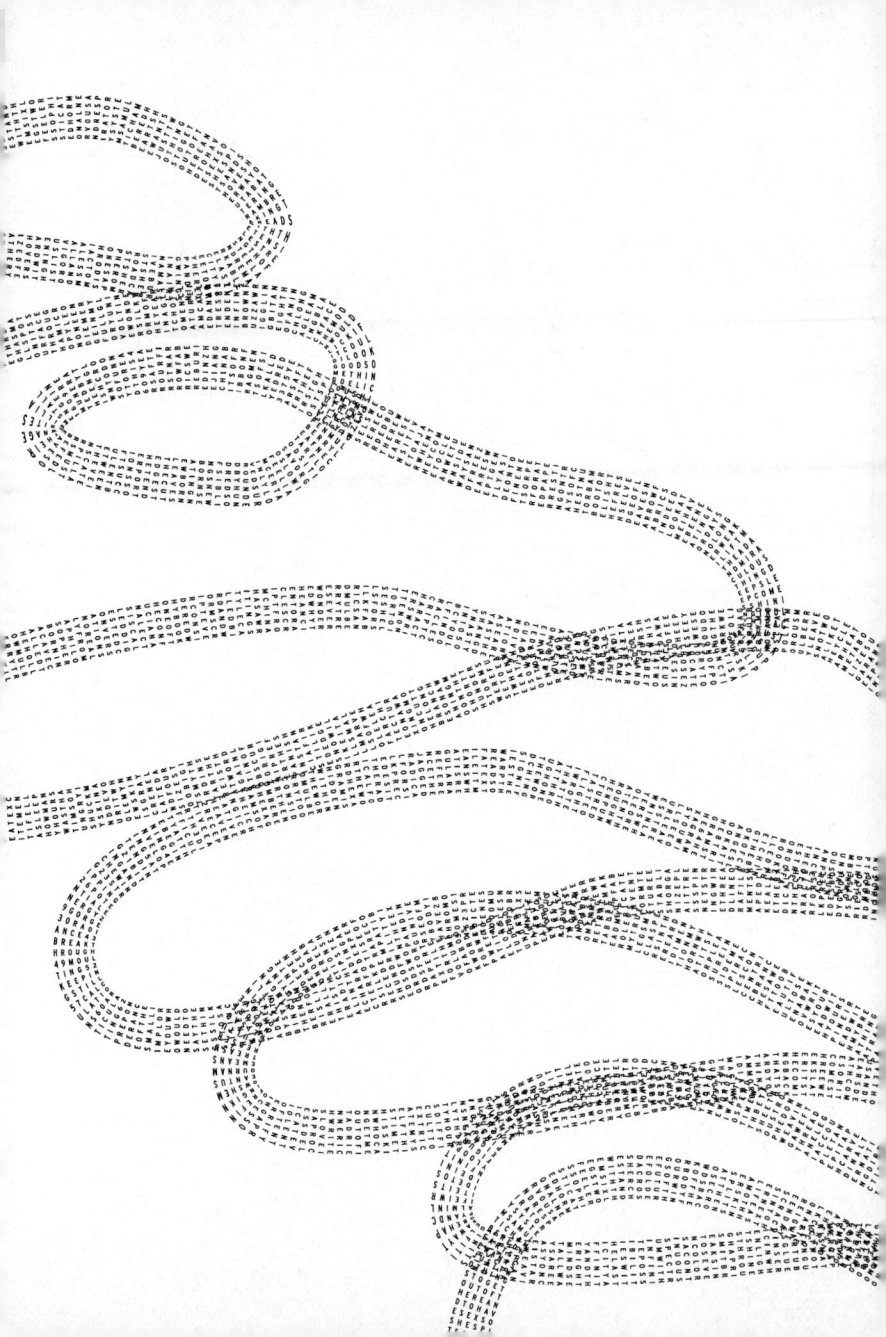

ITHOUGHT
YOUSHOULD

KNOW
HOWITIS

WITH
THE

CREATURES
WHOMADETHIS

OUR SHORT PRODUCTIVE LIVES

HOWOUR

MOTHER

BOMBYX

MORI

BOMB

FORSHORT

APUPA

INSIDEHER

SILK

COCOON

AFTER

EIGHTEEN

DAYS

CRACKS

INTO

HERNEXT

LIFE

ASAMOTH

HERSKIN

SPLITS

ATTHENOSE

CROWDSBACK

OFFHER

BODY

FOUR

WINGS

OFTHEFUTURE

FOLDED

ACROSS

HERCHEST

ANDWITHTHEM
SIXLEGS

TWOFEELERS
SOPHISTICATED

HORMONALNERVOUS
ANDRESPIRATORYSYSTEMS

AMULTICHAMBERED
HEART

SHEWANTSJUST

TWOTHINGS

TOGETOUTOFTHERE

ANDTOHAVESEX

SOSHE

SPITS

ANDSHOVES

HERWAYOUT

ABATTERING

RAMBREAKING

THREADSWITHTHETENSILE

STRENGTHOFSTEEL

ANDREMARKABLE

ELASTICITY

FREETODRYHEREXPANDING
WINGSINAIR

INAMASSIVE
BURST

SHEBROADCASTSHER
PHEROMONES

APHRODISIACTO

MALES

SMALLANDVIGOROUS

LISTENINGHARD

WITHOVERSIZED

FEATHERYANTENNAE

RIDICULOUSLYEAGER
THEYMAKETHEIRWAY

USINGCOMPOUNDEYES
KALEIDOSCOPIC

FROMKALOSBEAUTIFUL
ANDSKOPEINTOVIEW

SEEINGHER

EVERYWHERE

ANDBADLYWANTING

TOBESEEN

EVERYWHERE

BYHER

A TREMENDOUS FLUTTERING ENSUES

SOAWING

ISATHING

THATGETSYOU

THERE

TOTHEBLISS

OFBEING

TAILTOTAIL

FORHOURS

FIVETHOUSAND

YEARS

MALEOR

FEMALE

ALLTHATFUSS

ABOUTNOTFLYING

IFWEMATE

WEAREALL

CALLED

QUEENS

ANEW

MOTHER

DOESNOTHING

HALFWAY

SHESWELLS

FLUFFYBELLIED

GREATWITHEGGS

THREETOFIVEHUNDRED

THESIZEOF

SESAMESEEDS

THEYSPILLFORTH
INTWOBATCHES

AFEWHOURS
RESTBETWEEN

STICKYANDGOLDEN
THEYLODGE

ALLOVERTHE
COCOON

HEALTHYEGGS

TURNFROM

YOLKGOLD

TOBLUISH

BLACK

INTENDAYS

INACOOL

DRY

PLACE

THEEGGS

CANGO

DORMANT

UPTO

TENMONTHS

TOBEREVIVED

INAPOUCHWARMED

BETWEENTHE

BREASTSOFAWOMAN

ORLETSBEHONEST

AHEATEDROOM

INIDEAL

CONDITIONS

THEEGGS

STARTINCUBATING

WHENTHEBUDS

ONTHEMULBERRY

ARETWO

CENTIMETERSLONG

SOITBEGINS

FIRSTINSTAR

MYOWNEGG

TREMBLES

STICKYSOFT

IEATAHOLE

THROUGH

ASMALLSPOT

ONITSSURFACE

THROUGHA

MICROPYLE

ON

ONE

END

IEMERGE

INMYFULLGLORY

UNIVOLTINE

WONDER

SILKWORM

OFTHEYEAR

INAGLITCHOF

NOMENCLATURE

IAMCALLEDAN

ANT

RESPLENDENT

INFINEBROWNFUZZ

AWRIGGLINGBIT

ANEIGHTH

OFAN

INCHLONG

AGLEAMINGBLACK

FACETHEMOON

WOULDLICKIFITCOULD

ILOOKGOOD

SOMETHING

DELICIOUS

HITSMYMOUTH

INSTINCTIVELYIOPEN

MULBERRYLEAF

NECTARFLOODSIT

ISAVOR

GOSLOW

IFEELIAM

CERTAINLYLOVED

SURROUNDEDBY

HUNDREDSOFSIBLINGS

NEWBORNSEATING

NEWBORNLEAVES

THECUT

EDGES

THE

TENDERPORTIONS

SOFTSUCCULENT

BETWEENTHEVEINS

CATERPILLARS

MUSTBEFED

LEAVESOF

THEIROWNAGE

WRITES

WILLIAMSTALLENGE

IN1609

REMUNERATED

BYTHEENGLISHCROWN

TODOSO

FUNNYTO

READTHIS

4609YEARS

AFTER

OURFIRST

NARROWFABRICS

WEREBURIEDIN

ZHEJIANGCHINA

BITSOFRIBBON

FRAGMENTSOFSILK

ALLDYED

RED

3375YEARSAFTER
THEFIRSTGHOSTS

PIECESOFSILK
IMPRINTEDON

BRONZEVESSELS
WERERECORDED

BUT

HEREWEARE

SENSITIVETO

AJAR

WHENTHEYCOME

TOCLEAN

WETURN

SIDEWAYSANDFREEZE

ARESWEPTGENTLYASIDE
ONTOFINENETSOR

PERFORATEDPAPER
RESTINGON

TRAYSOFCHESTNUT
ORBAMBOO

TORELISH

THEFRESH

SELVAGE

OFLEAVES

NARROWFABRICS

INDEED

LOOKATME

IHAVEBEEN

EATING

FORDAYS

NOLONGER

WEAK

ILIFTMYHEAD

AND

MIRACULOUS

THING

DEEPSLEEP

COMESSHINING

TRULYMIRACULOUSTHING

WAKINGUP

WESLIP

OURSKIN

ITISAFUNCTIONOFPOETRY
TOLOCATE

THOSEZONES
INSIDEUS

THATWOULDBE
FREE
ANDDECLARE
THEMSO

WRITESCD
WRIGHT

AREYOUSURPRISED

IQUOTEAPOET

DONTBE

WEINVENTEDLANGUAGE

INDIVINATIONS

ASEARLYAS

THESHANGDYNASTY

IN1050BC

YOULLFIND

ORACLESCRIPT

CHARACTERS
WRITTEN

ONTORTOISE
SHELLSFOR

SILKFABRICSAND
MULBERRYTREES

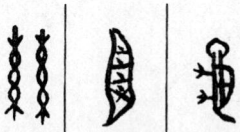

silk | silkworm | tortoise

EVERWONDEREDWHY
THEANCIENTORACLE

SCRIPTFROMCHINA
HASAWRITINGSTYLE

CALLEDBIRDAND
WORMSCRIPT

EVERCONSIDEREDWHY

BOOKONEOF

THECONFUCIAN

ANALECTS

ISCALLEDDIGESTED

CONVERSATIONS

NO

REALLY

FROMAPHILOSOPHER

BORNINA

CAVECALLEDTHE

HOLLOWMULBERRYTREE

WHENIHAVEPRESENTEDONECORNER
OFASUBJECTTOANYONEANDHE

CANNOTLEARNFROMITTHEOTHER
THREEIDONOTREPEATMYLESSON

MULBERRYTRANSLATESUS

WETRANSLATEIT

LOOKTHERADICALFORSILK

ISINTHEWORD

SCRIPTURE
經文

OK

EMBARRASSEDTOSAY

INMYGREATEXCITEMENT

IFELLASLEEP

HOWMANYHOURS

WASTHAT

IMSOHUNGRYI

SHUCKMYSKIN

ANDDEVOUR

ITWHOLE

MYNEWSKIN

ISGRAY

CRENELLATED

AND

FOURSIZES

TOOBIG

ITSMYTHIRD

INSTAR

THEREIS

THATWORDAGAIN

LATINOF

OBSCUREORIGIN

IPREFERTHESPANISH

INSTANCIA

TO

URGE

FIRSTILIKEDEDGES

NOWILIKEITALL

SMALLMARVELSOF

WHOLELEAFARCHITECTURE

ONAWAXINGMOON

CUTTHELONGBRANCHES

ONAWANINGMOON

THESHORT

THUNDERSTORMS
WEREFUSETOEAT

WHENWEEAT
THESOUNDOF

TORRENTIALRAIN
PLAYINGONLEAVES

WECANTSTAND

STRONGSMELLS

LIKEIT

SWEETANDCLEAN

OURSHITWHISKEDAWAY

TOFEEDSHEEP

WESEEYOU

WESEEYOUDOINGTHEWORK

WEARE

OLIGOPHAGUS

MULBERRY

MONOGAMOUS

LEAF

POLYAMOROUS

MULBERRY

LEAVESNO

TWOALIKE

THEYCLEARHEAT

METABOLIZESUGAR

ANDEXPELWIND

WELOVETHEM

COOLEDINTHESHADE

INSATIABLE

VORACIOUS

IEATTOOMUCH

BUTITSJUSTSOGOOD

CHEW

SIDEWAYS

INTHOUSANDS

OFARCS

INDIZZYING

DETAIL

ENOUGHTOWRITE

THEGREATESTBOOK

ONMULBERRICULTURE

WHICHREMINDSME

ASILKMANUSCRIPT

FOUNDINATOMB

INMOUNTAINOUS

HUNANPROVINCE

ISTHEOLDEST

RECORD

OFABOOK

CALLED

THEICHING

易經

THEBOOKOF

CHANGES

LOOK

ATTHE

8TRIGRAMS

THE64HEXAGRAMS

YOUWILL

SEE

OURLEAVES
STREWNINLAYERS

WHOLEOR
EATENTHROUGH

WHENPUNCTURED
TASTEOFLIGHT

IWROTETHAT
THROUGHONE

THEWORDCHING

經

SIGNIFIESTHEWARP

THREADSOFATEXTILE

ITMEANSWHATISREGULAR

AREFERENCE

THEJAGGEDRADICAL

糸

FORSILK

PRECEDESIT

CONSIDERTHE

HEXAGRAMS

OFTHE

ICHING

1CREATIVEHEAVEN

2RECEPTIVEEARTH

3DIFFICULTY

ATTHEBEGINNING

4ENVELOPING

5ATTENDING

21BITINGANDCHEWING

23STRIPPING

26POTENTIAL
ENERGY

29GORGE

30RADIANCE

43BREAKTHROUGH

49MOULTING

52KEEPINGSTILL

57CALCULATIONS

60ARTICULATING

62PREPONDERANCEOFTHESMALL

IIMPLOREYOU

WHO

WOULDNEEDTOSAY

THESETHINGS

SILK

SI

TOSAYITINCHINESE

WITHTHEWRONGTONE

ISADEATHBY

STABBING

ISTHENUMBER

FOUR

ISLITERALLY

THIS

THERADICAL
INTHECHARACTERFOR

SILK
絲

PRECEDES
HUNDREDSOFWORDS

WORDSFORPAPER
紙

TEXTILE
紡織品

FORTHEVOLUMEOFABOOK
編

WORDSFORWARP
經

WEFT
緯線

LATITUDE
緯度

LONGITUDE
經度

PARALLEL
緯線

ROUTE
線路

WORDSLIKECOMPILE
編

COMPOSE
組成

EDIT
編輯

WEAVE

編織

ARRANGE

編排

WRITE

編寫

MAKEUP

組成

FABRICATEINVENT

編造

FORMTEXTUREESTABLISHORGANIZE

組織

PLAITTRESS

編

SPIN

紡

NET

STRING

WIRE

THREAD

LINEORA

FILAMENT

SHAPEDLIKEALINE

線

THERADICAL
INTHECHARACTER

FORSILK
PRECEDESBODY

GROUPSETSERIESCORD
組

ABIDING
IMMANENT

ORDINATE
CHANGELESS

CONSTANT
經

REVOLUTIONARYREVOLUTIONIST

THEOLDESTCOLOR

RED

紅

GOONCARRYONCONTINUEPROCEED

繼續

MANAGESTANDPASSTHROUGHENDURE

經

ADEFORMATION

形變

ADEATH

命終

SILKENSLIGHTESTSMALLEST
TRIFLINGTHELEAST

SLIGHTLYHARDLY
ALITTLE

ABIT
絲

IREARUP

ICALMDOWN

AFAT

LETTERL

CRASHEDOUT

MIDAIR

IUSEDTOCALLIT

DIAPAUSE

NOWCALLIT

TRANS

MOVING
INMYOLDSKIN

INSIDEIT
MYNEWSKIN

FEELSCLEARANDSHINY
FEELSEVERYTHING

INMYFOURTH

INSTAR

IKNOWMYTRUESKIN

ISTRANSFORMATION

MEDIUMAND

MATERIAL

THEYSAY
IHAVEASHORTLIFEBUT

IHAVEANEVENSHORTER
DEATH

IHAVESOMANY
ITPAINSME

IMAGINETHIS

FORFIVETHOUSANDYEARS

DEATHCOMESORIT

COMESTHREEWEEKSLATER

ITSTHECOMINGBACK

THATSHARD

YOUTHINK

IAMMORBIDIAM

IMAGINETHELANGUAGE

WRITTENINME

MEMENTO

MORI

MORUSALBA

MULBERRY

BOMBYXMORI

ME

MULBERRYMULBERRY

MULBERRY

IMOVESLOWLY

STARTFROMTHESIDE

THEFINEHAIRS

AREASHIVER

THROWMYHEAD

BACK

ANDLAUGH

ANDINLAUGHING

TRANS

NEARLYTHIRTYHOURS

DIFFICULTTO
EXTRICATEMYSELF

THISTIME
THISSKIN

WHOCANGETME
OUTOFIT

ADRIENNERICHWRITES
LOVEISAPROCESS

DELICATEVIOLENT
OFTENTERRIFYING

APROCESSOF
REFINING

IKNOWSHE
MEANTUS

OURNAMEMEANS

TREASURED

SERICULTURE

ISACULTUREOF

LOVE

ISAYINIT

OFLIVING

ANDDYING

OFINTERDEPENDENCE

HONORABLERELATIONSHIPS

TENDINGANDEXPERTISE

OFRARECOMPATIBILITY

INTHEEXPANDING

UNIVERSEOFMYBODY

IHAVE28CHROMOSOMES

14623PREDICTEDGENES

4000MUSCLES

NOTTOBRAG

SIXSIMPLEEYES

TOMAKEOUTLIGHT

AROBUSTTHORAXANDABDOMEN

MYRETRACTABLEHEAD

MYPROLEGSMYTRUELEGS

MYCLASPERSINTHEREAR

DIDIMENTIONMYHORN

WHATITSFOR

INSIDEME

SPIRACLES

CONCENTRICBRANCHES

AWEFT

TOOBEAUTIFUL

TOSEE

NABAKOVWRITES

YOUREADWITHYOURSPINE

IREADWITHMYBREATHING

ATRANSPARENTCHAINOFTUBES

NINEPAIRS

THEYFLOWER

ONEACHSIDEOFMYBODY
WITHEACHCONTRACTION

THEYCIRCULATE
DELICIOUSOXYGEN

INMOVEMENT

FRESHNESS

IAMFULLYFLEDGED

FATASAFINGER

PALESLATEBLUE

OYSTERWHITE

TENTHOUSANDTIMES

HEAVIER

THIRTYTIMES

LONGER

ABOUTTHIRTYDAYS

OLD

BUTWHOIS

COUNTING

ME

SILKWORMS

LOVE

TOCOUNT

ITCALMSMYNERVES

IGETRESTLESS

FIDGETY

STARTWANDERING

MYCHEST

GOESTRANSPARENT

ISHRINKALITTLE

PINKISH

THROW

MYHEADBACK

ANDFEEL

LIKE

IMGOING

TOTHROWUP

SILK

COMESSPUTTERINGOUT

JUSTBELOWMYMOUTH
MYSPINNERET

WORKS
NINEORTEN

INCHESINTHE
FIRSTMINUTE

SIXTYFIVEELLIPTICAL
MOTIONSMYHEADIS

SPINNING

THEBRIN

ISSUESIN

AGLUTINOUSSTATE

HARDENSINTOLINES

BECOMESSTRUCTURE

WITHSTRENGTHLENGTH
ANDLUSTER

THEFIBROINSTRANDS
EMERGEPRISMATIC

TWOTRIANGULARTUBES
GLUEDINSERICIN

WHENLIGHTSHINESTHROUGHAPRISM
ITBREAKSINTOSEVENCOLORS

ACONTINUOUSSPECTRUM
WITHINFINITEPOSSIBILITIES

WITHELASTICITYAFFINITY

ANDTHERIGHTMINDSET

ALLWAYS

AREEASY

ONCEISTARTWEAVING

ICANTHEAR

APRACTICE

ISNOTATHINGINITSELF

ITISAWAYTOBE

HAPPYANDCALMINLIFE

IWRITEIT

SIDETOSIDE

INFINITYLOOPS

FIGUREEIGHTSPINS

ASMUCHASSIXMILES

SIXTYHOURS

THREEDAYS

SUREICOUNT

IMODULATEIT

SLOWITDOWN

ELONGATETHELOOP

CONCENTRATEONTHELINE

ITRYNOTTOHAVEIDEAS

BECAUSETHEYREINACCURATE

INSTEADITRYTOTHINKOFTHEWORDS

IWANTTOSPENDTIMEWITH

BETASHEET

BOUSTROPHEDON

WEAVINGA

WEFTTHREAD

ANELEGIACCOUPLET

ANEPITAPH

CARVEDIN

ALTERNATINGDIRECTIONS

TOREVERSETHEREVERSE

BECOMESTHEWORK

TOSEPARATEYOURRIGHTBRAIN

FROMYOURLEFTANDBUILDBACKUP

TOREMOVESPECIFICOUTCOMESAND

TRULYCREATESOMETHING

SILK

LANGUAGE

MEDIUMS

INFINITELYLARGER

THAN

ANYINTENTION

THISLITTLE

SILKINME

POLYMATH

STRINGFIGURE

PRESENT

SMALLWILD

THINGSTHATSHINE

OBSTINATELY

HOLDTHEBODY

FREEFROMHARM

CLOTHTISSUE

BODYISSUE

HERE

ISTHISTHING

IMADEOFMYSELF

WITHOTHERS

ALIVE

INYOU

IGIVEYOUMY

繭

THISFLYINGGARMENT

FORTHESOUL

IVEDRAWN

INFINITY

INTO

IT

RESEARCH SAMPLER

The earliest human function of silk fabrics was wrapping children's bodies in the tomb. Inventory: a bundle of bright silk yarn thirty feet long in her hand. A billion-foot-long silk yarn for climbing to heaven.

•

In Madagascar during the Malagasy ritual of *famadihana*, ancestors' bones are exhumed from family crypts, celebrated with feasts and libations, dancing, and live music; they are offered prayers, blessings and consulted for guidance. Afterwards, their bodies are rewrapped singly or together in an ancestor bundle in freshly woven wild silk, and restored to the family crypt until the next celebration.

•

Ancient Chinese writings on silk were to communicate not only among humans, but between human and spiritual beings. Silk letters were tied to the foot of a wild goose. An ancient Chinese poem says, "calling to the boy to cook the carp, in its body a silk letter of one foot."

•

An excerpt from an ancient letter "protected by an inner wrapper of brown silk and an outer envelope of coarse fabric which bears instructions for the delivery of the letter" from a series found in a postbag in Dunhuang, China written in Sogdian, an Iranian language spoken in present day Uzbekistan: "Dear Sirs, It would be a good day for him who might see you happy and free from illness; and sirs, when I think of your good health, I consider *myself* immortal!"

•

A "book" of silk is a measure forty feet long, annotated on the selvage of ancient cloth. Other measures of silk include ells and aunes, mommies and piculs.

•

"I have often taken my little three inch brush prepared writing silk four feet in length, and gone off to inquire of different dialects," from a Chinese philosopher's letter in the first century.

•

In the second century, the Chinese Empress Teng, a lover of literature, asked only for chih, a paper made of waste silk, and ink cakes as royal gifts.

•

In the fourth century, the Chinese poet Su Hui wrote a reversible poem in five colors of silk, designed to correspond to a star gauge for reading the cosmos. Her poem had nearly eight thousand possible readings. Su Hui sent this poem as a letter to her husband who was far away. Upon reading Su Hui's poem, the couple reunited for life.

•

Throughout the Muslim world there is a strong belief in the protective power of the written word in the Koran. Between the eighth and the twelfth century, single, horizon-like inscriptions were written on tiraz (from *tarz*, Persian for embroidery), in Arabic letters embroidered in silk on a linen or cotton ground. The writing honored the prophet Mohammed, named the commissioning caliphate, said where and when the cloth was woven, and blessed and protected the recipient of the cloth. Sometimes a stray blessing from the weaver was appended.

•

In the Koran, paradise is conceived as a place of silken cushions and carpets. The prophet Mohammed is said to have remarked that he who wears silk in this life shall forgo it in the next. Mulham, with a silk warp and a cotton weft, was sometimes permitted, as only the cotton touched the body.

•

Bolts of Byzantine silk were held up as barriers for the crowd or unfurled as ground covering for a royal return. One kissed the hem of the Sultan's robe.

•

Heavily embroidered West African riga or robes of honor, magical and protective, especially in times of war, create an effect of bigness. "The older the silk embroideries get the shinier they will become. Your gown will tear while the embroidery remains intact."

•

"I am dying by inches from lack of any body to talk to about worms." Mary Ruefle's paraphrase of correspondence from Charles Darwin to William Darwin Fox.

•

Vladimir Nabokov, in his novel *Transparent*: "the spine is the true reader's main organ." In a private letter to Archibald MacLeish, he writes: "there is that movement of light in one of your most famous poems that invariably sends a shiver of delight up and down my spine whenever I think of it."

•

Emily Dickinson's letter to Susan Dickinson, manuscript A637. "Tis a dange / rous moment / for any one / when the meaning / goes out of things / and Life stands / Straight – and / punctual X and / yet no contents / signal / comes / Yet such mo / ments are / If we survive / them they expand / us, if we do / not, but that / is Death X, whose / if is Everlasting / when I was a / little girl I called / the Cemetery / Tarrytown / but now I call it Trans – / A wherefore / but no more / And X the if / of Diety – Avalanche / or Avenue – Every / Heart asks which" Note: the X's are variant strains or alternate reading paths in the poem draft. "Contents" or "signal" are variant, as is the phrasing that begins with "whose if is Everlasting" and "the if of Diety."

•

Agnes Martin: I try not to have ideas because they're inaccurate

•

Dianna Frid: I try to think of the words I want to spend time with

•

Cecilia Vicuña: To reverse the reverse becomes the work

•

Marta Werner: It is so hard to let go of contextualization

•

Fiorenzo Omenetto: separate your right brain from your left, and build back up

•

Rosmarie Waldrop: language, a medium infinitely larger than any intention

•

Franck André Jamme's translation of a tantra painting: small wild / things that shine /obstinately

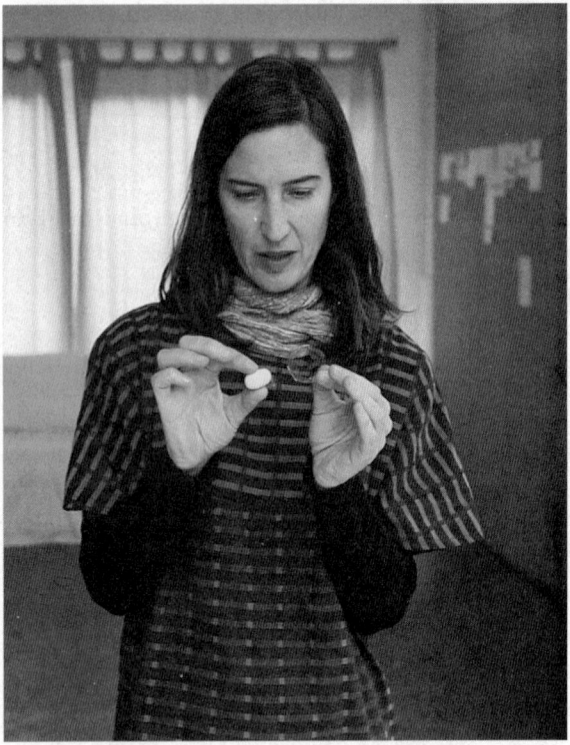

Jen Bervin holding a silk cocoon and a silk film from Tufts at Montalvo Art Center, 2016. Photo by Charlotte Lagarde.

PROJECT NOTE

Silk, as a material, is compatible with body tissues; our immune system accepts it on surfaces as sensitive as the human brain.

In 2010, I visited Tufts University's Bioengineering Department, where David Kaplan and Fiorenzo Omenetto were reinventing silk as a cutting-edge technological material in a new form: reverse-engineered liquefied silk. One facet of their remarkable research captured my attention: a silk biosensor in development, written nanoscale on clear silk film. It was designed to be implanted in the body to sense shifts in target materials—blood sugar in hemoglobin, for example. The meaningful health context, the scale of the writing, and the simplicity of the material astounded me.

This type of film, due to its optical nature, can be read as a projection with fiber optic light. When I projected the test film in Fio's office, the clip art on the prototype I saw there gave me pause—the content gap really surprised me. I thought, if it is possible to write in that context—inside the body, on silk, at that scale, I wanted to think further about what else might be inscribed there.

I empathized with the sensor's future "reader," and imagined people with the sensor inside of them, in the anxiety-provoking space of monitoring it for abnormal changes in their health. I wanted to create something akin to a talisman, a powerful text hidden on the body to protect the wearer.

The poem is essentially a love poem. As I wrote it from the perspective of a silkworm, I often

thought of a quote I read by a Japanese weaver:
My clothes are my body, I do not loan them out.
If I give them, I give them for good.

As an artist and writer, I often take a research-driven approach to create interdisciplinary works that combine text and textiles. When most people think of textiles, they think of clothes. But textiles can cross boundaries: my first weaving teacher created woven designs for heart valves. Silk has a rich 5,000 year-old international cultural history. In thinking about what might be meaningfully written on a silk sensor inside the body, I became interested in which aspects of silk's history a sensor might encode and why.

My journey to create *Silk Poems* spanned six years, and developed with help and expertise from thirty international textile archives, medical libraries,

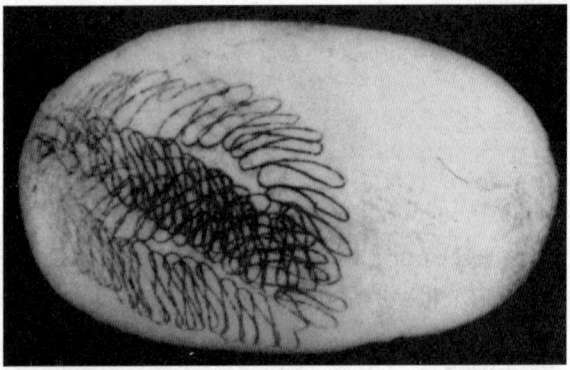

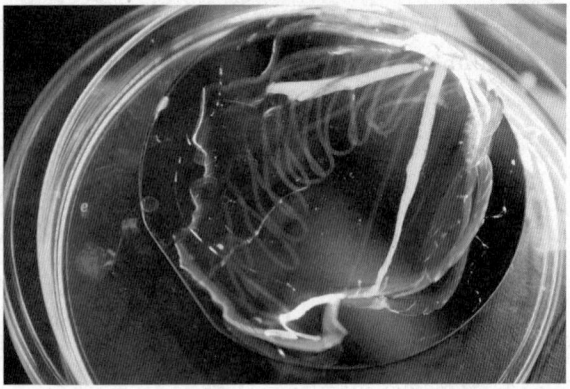

TOP: Silkworm patterned filament in the cocoon, Japan 2016. BOTTOM: Fabrication view of *Silk Poems* at Tufts University, version four, nanoimprinted gold spatter on a 3.5 inch silk film, 2016.

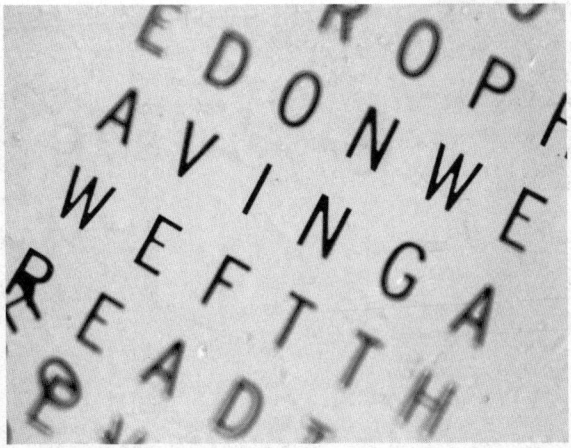

Silk Poem strand suspended in silk film, microscopic view of gold letters. Photo by Bradley Napier.

nanotechnology and biomedical labs, and sericulture sites in North America, Europe, the Middle East, and Asia, thanks to a major grant from Creative Capital for this project.

The form of the poem strand is modeled on silk at the DNA level—the six-character repeat in the genome is the basis for the six letter enjambed line of the strand; the shape of the strand reflects both the filament pattern silkworms enact when writing

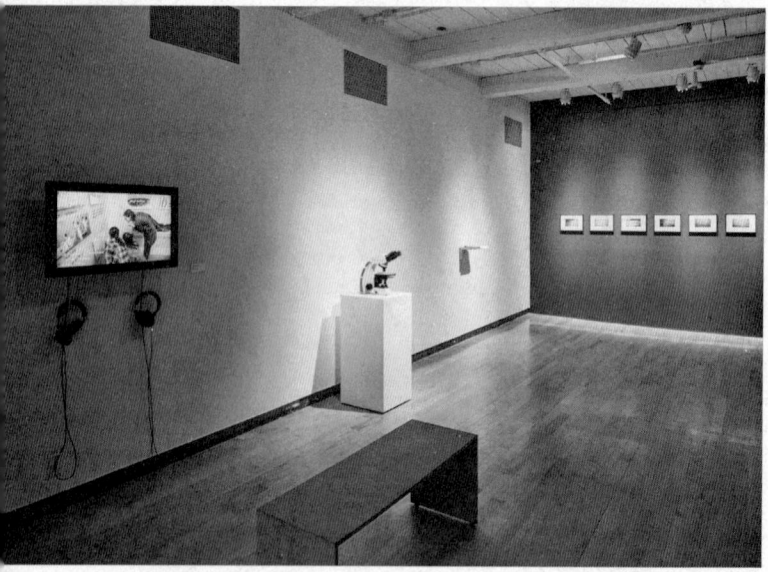

Installation view, *Explode Every Day: An Inquiry into the Phenomena of Wonder*, MASS MoCA, North Adams, Massachusetts, 2016. Photo by Tony Luong.

their cocoon, and silk's beta sheet, which forms like the weft thread in a weaving.

In 2016, at Tufts University's Department of Biomedical Engineering, we were able to fabricate the poem I wrote on silk film, thanks to the generosity of Fiorenzo Omenetto and the patience of Bradley Napier through the various trials. They used a mask to etch the poem in gold spatter on a wafer and poured liquid silk over it. When the silk dried, the letters were suspended in the film.

Silk Poems premiered in the year-long exhibition *Explode Every Day: An Inquiry into the Phenomena of Wonder,* curated by Denise Markonish and Sean Foley at MASS MoCA, from May 2016 to March 2017. In it, the poem in silk film was viewed through a microscope, accompanied by a video about the research process by Charlotte Lagarde, and a reading version of *Silk Poems*.

In the margin of this book, a tiny version of the poem strand accrues progressively, apace with reading. Bob Brown's *Words* (1931) was the first place I saw something like this, and I still marvel at how his poems disappear in plain sight, even when you're looking for them.

JEN BERVIN

ACKNOWLEDGMENTS

Thank you to the outstanding staff, grantees, and supporters of Creative Capital, past and present, for nourishing this work. *Silk Poems* received major support from a 2013 Creative Capital Grant in Literature, and additional in-kind support from Bogliasco Foundation, MASS MoCA, The Josef and Anni Albers Foundation, Brown University Literary Arts, Montalvo Art Center's Lucas Artist Program, Elizabeth Willis, The Camargo Foundation, and the Robert Rauschenberg Foundation.

Special and huge thanks to Fiorenzo Omenetto and David Kaplan at the Tufts University Bioengineering Department's Silk Lab, and to Amanda Schaffer, for your vast agile minds, and for inspiring and welcoming this work.

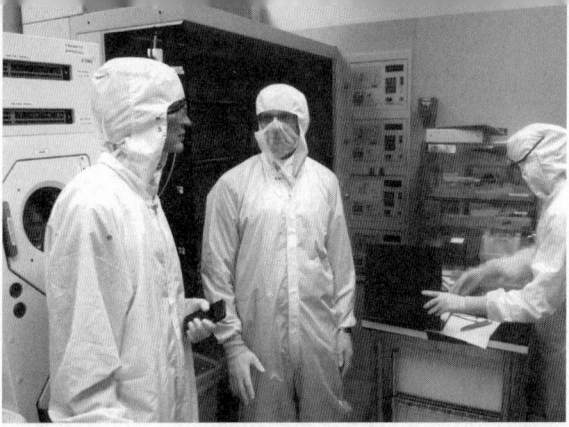

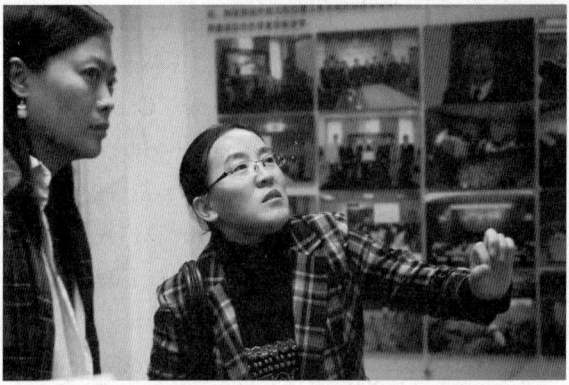

TOP: Jen Bervin and Ed Myers, Stanford University Nanofabrication Facility, Palo Alto, California, 2012.
BOTTOM: Huang Haisu and Dr. Tieling Xing, Soochow University Silk Engineering Department, Suzhou, China, 2013.

Thank you, Charlotte Lagarde, for traveling the world with me to document this project, and for your remarkable gifts as a filmmaker, artist, and storyteller. Thanks for your support on all fronts. Your love, strength, companionship, humor and guidance sustain and inspire me.

Thank you Vamsi Yadavalli at Virginia Commonwealth University's Department of Chemical and Life Science Engineering, for experimenting with new trials of *Silk Poems* using a silk fibroin photolith technique in trials as small as the thumbnails in this book.

My gratitude for your expertise on the research trail to: Stanford University Nanofabrication Facility; Eva Labson, Assistant Manager, Antonio Ratti Textile Center, The Metropolitan Museum of Art; Karla Nielsen, Curator of Literature, Columbia

University Rare Books and Manuscript Library; Columbia University Starr East Asian Library; Fashion Institute of Technology Library; The Mütter Museum and Historical Medical Library; Stan Gorski, Special Collections Librarian, Gutman Library, and Marcella Milio, Curator, Paley Design Center, Philadelphia University; Nancy Kuhl, Curator, Beinecke Rare Books and Manuscript Library, Yale University, New Haven; Carol Bier, The Textile Museum, Washington D.C.; Musée des Tissus et Arts Décoratifs de Lyon, France; Maison des Canuts, Lyon; Institut du Monde Arabe, Paris; Bibliothèque des Arts Décoratifs, Paris; Silk Hakubutsukan, Yokohama, Japan; Japanese translation: Miwako Ozawa; Tokyo National Museum; Kyoto Municipal Museum of Traditional Crafts; Orinasu-Kan Museum, Kyoto; Nishijin Textile Center, Kyoto; Metersbonwe Museum, Shanghai, China; Chinese translation: Huang Haisu; Dr. Tieling Xing, Soochow University Silk Engineering Department, Suzhou; Suzhou Silk Museum; Suzhou Embroidery Research Institute; The China National Silk Museum, Hangzhou; Qiaoxian Yu, Jiangang Yu, Yuhui Mei, and Tongyao Yu, Silkworm Farm, Tongxiang, China; The International Dunhuang Project, Dunhuang, China; The Liguria Study Center, Bogliasco, Italy; Francina Chiara, La Fondazione Antonio Ratti Textile Museum and Library, Como; Museo Didattico della Seta, Como; Frederica Centulani, Palazzo Mocenigo Library, Venice; Biblioteca Statale di Lucca; Topkapi Saray Muzesi Archive, Istanbul, Turkey; and Chuka Kuprava, State Silk Museum, Tbilisi, Georgia.

Thank you for your help and generosity:

Kenny Fries, Sawako Nakayasu, Jonathan Way, Xu Xi, Miho Kinnas, Jen Hyde, David Perry, Monika Lin, Arthur Solway, Violet Feng, Wang Mingjie, Laura Harrison, Mei-Yin Ng, Lydia Matthews, and Ayşe Aydoğan. For studio research assistance, deep thanks to Claudia Markey and Lauren Woodard.

I am grateful to the poet Yolanda Arroyo Pizarro for teaching me the Nigerian proverb in San Juan, Puerto Rico; to Allie Foradas, curator at MASS MoCA for introducing me to the Nabokov quote; and to Bibiche Lagarde for recounting counting; to the writers C.D. Wright, Cecilia Vicuña, Marta Werner, Rosmarie Waldrop, Franck André Jamme, and Tsuen-Hsuin Tsien. Tsien's book, *Written on Bamboo and Silk* (University of Chicago) is the source of the oracle script on page 53, and is quoted throughout the book. Though rooted in research and intertextuality, *Silk Poems* is also invented, playful and speculative.

Deeply talented people designed this work and are to be roundly thanked. The poem strand and manuscript draft for the show at MASS MoCA was typeset by Heather Watkins. Paul Jordan of Bark Frameworks fine-tuned the microscope to hold the poem in the exhibition. Jeff Clark empathetically translated the manuscript into book form. Lindsey Boldt fielded all aspects of this manuscript expertly at Nightboat Books. I'm indebted to Stephen Motika, for the great work you do at Nightboat, Poets House, and on the page, and for championing my work as an artist and teacher for over a decade. It's a joy to join the many authors I admire in the Nightboat Books family.

Thank you Jody Gladding for the close feedback

and essential dialogue on the poem. For sustaining conversations, guidance, and support, thank you Dianna Frid, Mary Ruefle, Denise Markonish, Karen Emmerich, Elizabeth Willis, Cole Swensen, Nancy Kuhl, Helen Mirra, Joanna Howard, Catherine McRae, Elizabeth Zuba, and Francesca Capone.

Thank you to friends and publishers Anna Moschovakis and Matvei Yankelevich of Ugly Duckling Presse, Steve Clay of Granary Books, Christine Burgin and New Directions for your longstanding support.

Thank you to the professors, journalists, curators, institutions, and conferences for your support of this work and to transformative readers, audiences, and communities: past, present and future.

FURTHER READING

Douny, Laurence. "Silk-embroidered garments as transformative processes: Layering, inscribing and displaying Hausa material identities." *Journal of Material Culture* 16 (2011): 401–415. (Referenced on p. 160.)

Feltwell, John. *The Story of Silk.* New York: St. Martins Press, 1991. (Referenced on pp. vii, 25, 37.)

Kusimba, Chapurukha Makokha. *Unwrapping the Textile Traditions of Madagascar.* Los Angeles: UCLA Fowler Museum of Cultural History Textile Series, 2005. (Referenced on p. 155.)

Tsien, Tsuen-hsuin. *Written on Bamboo and Silk: The Beginnings of Chinese Books and Inscriptions.* Chicago: University of Chicago Press, 1962. (Image credit p. 53; referenced on pp. 51–53, 156–157.)

Xinru, Liu. *Silk and Religion. An Exploration of Material Life and the Thought of People A.D. 600–1200.* Delhi: Oxford University Press, 1998. (Referenced on pp. 158–159.)

NIGHTBOAT BOOKS, a nonprofit organization, seeks to develop audiences for writers whose work resists convention and transcends boundaries. We publish books rich with poignancy, intelligence, and risk. Please visit our website, www.nightboat.org, to learn about our titles and how you can support our future publications.

The following individuals have supported the publication of this book. We thank them for their generosity and commitment to the mission of Nightboat Books:

ELIZABETH MOTIKA

BENJAMIN TAYLOR

In addition, this book has been made possible, in part, by grants from the National Endowment for the Arts and the New York State Council on the Arts Literature Program.

ART WORKS. | National Endowment for the Arts arts.gov | NEW YORK STATE OF OPPORTUNITY. | Council on the Arts